GUITAR PRAISE!

75 Contemporary
Favorites
for
Guitar-driven
Worship

ARRANGED
BY
ED HOGAN

LILLENAS
PUBLISHING COMPANY

BAREFOOT
MINISTRIES

Kansas City, MO 64141

MUSIC has a way of shaping us, of moving us. It penetrates our minds, hearts, and emotions. Music digs into our very being and often can define who we are. For Christians, the music we sing and listen to even affects our spiritual walk. Authentic praise sung to God draws us closer to him, dispels our fears and doubt, lifts our states of mind. It's true that God inhabits the praises of his people.

Matthew 28:19 records Jesus giving what we now call *The Great Commission*. "Therefore, go and make disciples of all nations..." (NIV) The Church is not called to be sedentary, sitting idle as we wait for His return. We are commanded to make disciples who are thirsty for spiritual water. Genuine discipleship involves much more than convincing someone to make a decision for Christ. That is simply where the discipleship begins. Jesus spent three years teaching His disciples, walking with them, laughing with them, crying, sleeping, and eating with them. He spent three years training those men to become the leaders of the Church. If Jesus spent that much time with his discipleship program, shouldn't we do likewise?

No Limits is a new line of products from Barefoot Ministries designed to help teens and young adults to do exactly that, become disciples of Christ. As music plays such a giant part in our lives, Lillenas Publishing Company and Barefoot Ministries have teamed up to create GUITAR PRAISE!, part of the *No Limits* product line. GUITAR PRAISE! is a collection of the most popular praise songs today, songs that draw us closer to God and strengthen our spiritual walk. Designed for use with guitar or praise bands, it features notated melodies, lyrics, and chords, and are arranged in "guitar friendly" keys. We trust our efforts will bless you, your ministry, and help you become a stronger disciple of Jesus.

Blessings!

Lillenas Publishing Company
Barefoot Ministries

1   Let Everything That Has Breath

Words and Music by
MATT REDMAN

With energy ♩ = ca. 120

Let ev-'ry-thing— that,   ev-'ry-thing— that,   ev-'ry-thing— that

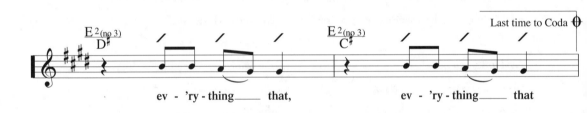

has— breath,   praise   the Lord.   Let ev-'ry-thing— that,

ev-'ry-thing— that,   ev-'ry-thing— that

has— breath,   praise   the Lord._____

1. Praise— You in the morn-ing,   praise— You in the ev-'ning,
2. Praise— You in the heav-ens.   Join - ing with the an-gels,

Praise___ You when I'm young and when I'm old._____
Prais - ing You for-ev - er and a day._____

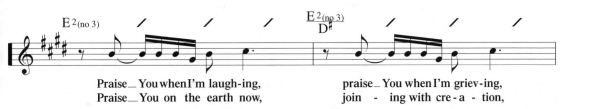

Praise___ You when I'm laugh-ing,   praise___ You when I'm griev-ing,
Praise___ You on the earth now,   join - ing with cre-a - tion,

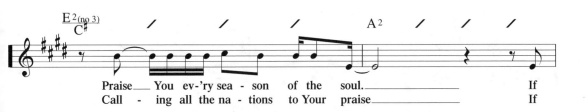

Praise___ You ev-'ry sea - son of the soul._____   If
Call - ing all the na - tions to Your praise_____   If

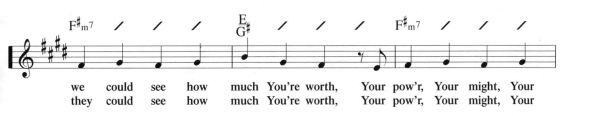

we could see how much You're worth, Your pow'r, Your might, Your
they could see how much You're worth, Your pow'r, Your might, Your

end - less love, then sure - ly we would nev - er cease to
end - less love, then sure - ly they would nev - er cease to

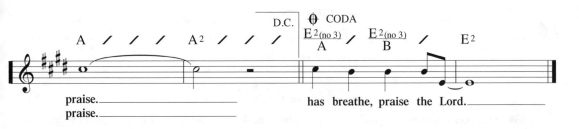

praise._____
praise._____   has breathe, praise the Lord._____

Praise___ You when I'm young and when I'm old.___
Prais - ing You for - ev - er and a day.___

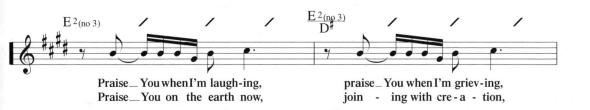

Praise___ You when I'm laugh-ing,   praise___ You when I'm griev-ing,
Praise___ You on the earth now,   join - ing with cre - a - tion,

Praise___ You ev-'ry sea - son of the soul.___   If
Call - ing all the na - tions to Your praise___   If

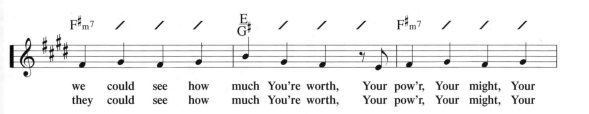

we could see how much You're worth, Your pow'r, Your might, Your
they could see how much You're worth, Your pow'r, Your might, Your

end - less love, then sure - ly we would nev - er cease to
end - less love, then sure - ly they would nev - er cease to

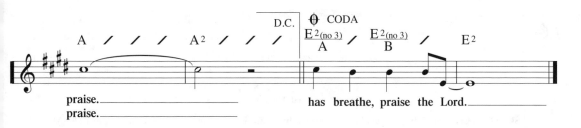

praise.___
praise.___   has breathe, praise the Lord.___

2 Draw Me Close

Words and Music by
KELLY CARPENTER

Gently ♩ = ca. 76

Draw me close___ to You,

nev - er let___ me go.

I lay it all___ down a - gain,___

to hear You say___ that I'm Your friend.___

You are my___ de - sire,

no one else___ will do,

'Cause noth - ing else — could take Your place, —————————

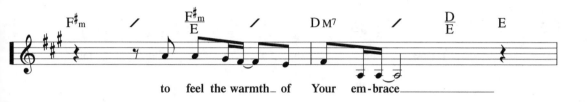

to feel the warmth — of Your em - brace —————————

Help me find — the way, bring me back — to

You. ————————————— You're all — I want, —————————

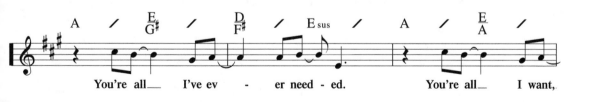

You're all — I've ev - er need - ed. You're all — I want,

————————— help me know You are near. —————————

3

How Deep the Father's Love for Us

Words and Music by
STUART TOWNEND

With feeling ♩ = ca. 94

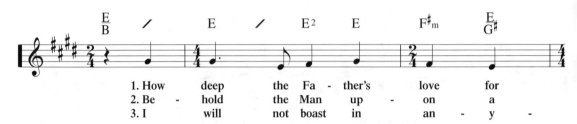

1. How deep the Fa - ther's love for
2. Be - hold the Man up - on a
3. I will not boast in an - y -

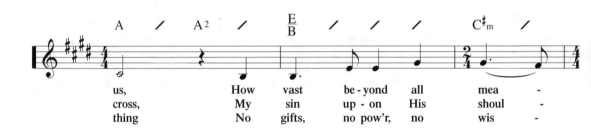

us, How vast be - yond all mea -
cross, My sin up - on His shoul -
thing No gifts, no pow'r, no wis -

sure; That He should give His on - ly
ders; A - shamed I hear my mock - ing
dom; But I will boast in Je - sus

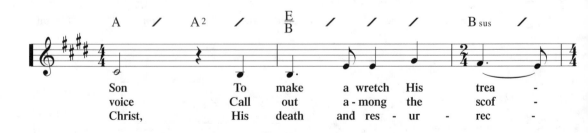

Son To make a wretch His trea -
voice Call out a - mong the scof -
Christ, His death and res - ur - rec -

sure.   How great the pain of fear - ing
fers.   It was my sin that held Him
tion.   Why should I gain from His re -

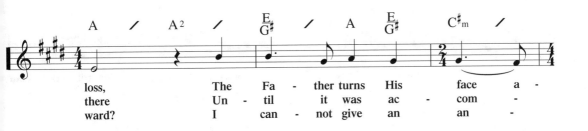

loss,   The Fa - ther turns His face a -
there   Un - til it was ac - com -
ward?   I can - not give an an -

way   As wounds which mar the Cho - sen
plished;   His dy - ing breath has brought me
swer.   But this I know with all my

One,   Bring man - y sons to glo - ry.
life   I know that it is fin - ished.
heart;   His wounds have paid my ran - som.

4

Shout to the Lord

Words and Music by
DARLENE ZSCHECH

With vigor ♩ = ca. 80

My Je - sus, my Sav - ior, Lord, there is none___ like___ You;___

___ All of my days___ I want to praise___ the won-ders of Your

might - y love. My com - fort, my Shel - ter,

Tow-er of ref - uge and strength;___ Let ev-'ry breath,___ all that I am,___

___ nev-er cease to wor - ship You.

Shout to the Lord,___ all the earth,___ let us sing___

5

Did You Feel
the Mountains Tremble?

Words and Music by
MARTIN SMITH

PLEASE NOTE: Copying of this product is NOT covered by CCLI licenses. For CCLI information call 1-800-234-2446.

6

Awesome in This Place

Words and Music by
DAVE BILLINGTON

Reverently ♩ = ca. 62

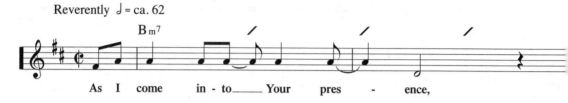

As I come in-to___ Your pres - ence,

past the gates___ of praise,_____ in - to Your sanc - tu - ar -

- y_____ till we're stand - ing face___ to face;_____ I

look up - on_____ Your coun - te - nance, I see the

full - ness of___ Your grace,_____ and I can on - ly bow down___

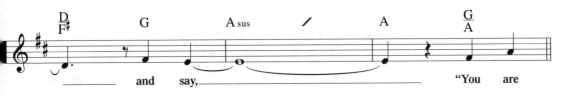

and say, "You are

awe - some in____ this place,_____ Might - y God,_____

_____ You are awe - some in____ this place,_____ Ab - ba

Fa - ther;_____ You are wor - thy of____ all praise,

_____ to You our lives____ we raise,_____ You are

awe - some in____ this place,_____ Might - y____ God."_____

7   Cry of My Heart

Words and Music by
TERRY BUTLER

PLEASE NOTE: Copying of this product is NOT covered by CCLI licenses. For CCLI information call 1-800-234-2446.

He Is Lord

Anonymous
Arranged by Ed Hogan

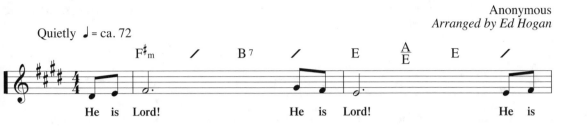

He is Lord! He is Lord! He is

ris - en from the dead and He is Lord!_____ Ev - 'ry

knee shall bow, ev - 'ry tongue con - fess That

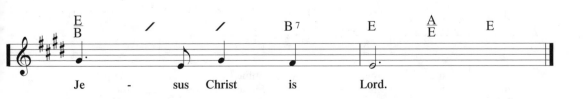

Je - sus Christ is Lord.

9   Shine, Jesus, Shine

Words and Music by
GRAHAM KENDRICK

With fervor ♩ = ca. 96

1. Lord, the light of Your love is shin - ing,
2. Lord, I come to Your awe - some pres - ence,
3. As we gaze on Your king - ly bright - ness,

In the midst of the dark - ness shin - ing;
From the shad - ows in - to Your ra - diance;
So our fac - es dis - play Your like - ness,

Je - sus, Light of the world, shine up - on us,
By the blood I may en - ter Your bright - ness;
Ev - er chang - ing from glo - ry to glo - ry;

Set us free by the truth You now bring us;
Search me, try me, con - sume all my dark - ness;
Mir - rored here, may our lives tell Your sto - ry;

Shine on me. Shine on me.
Shine on me. Shine on me.
Shine on me. Shine on me.

Shine, Je - sus, shine,_____ fill this land with the

Fa - ther's glo - ry; Blaze, Spir - it, blaze,_____ set our

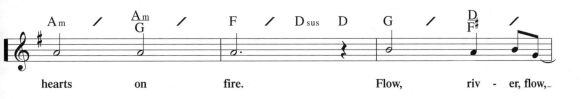

hearts on fire. Flow, riv - er, flow,_

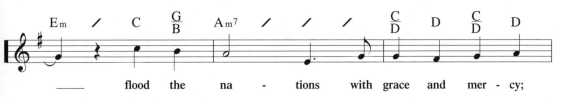

_____ flood the na - tions with grace and mer - cy;

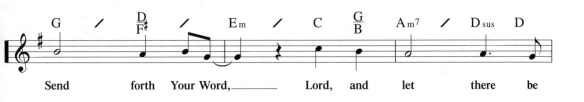

Send forth Your Word,_____ Lord, and let there be

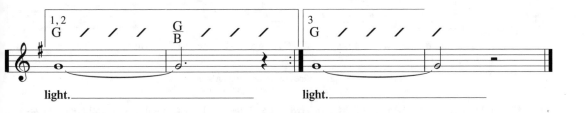

light._____ light._____

10 Holy and Anointed One

Words and Music by
JOHN BARNETT

Je - sus, Je -

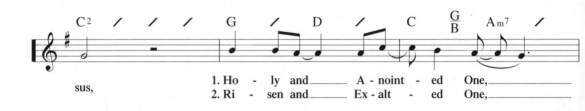

sus,
1. Ho - ly and___ A - noint - ed One,___
2. Ri - sen and___ Ex - alt - ed One,___

Je - sus sus Your Name is like hon -

- ey on___ my___ lips,___ Your Spir-it like wa - ter to___ my___ soul.

Your Word is a lamp un - to my feet; Je-sus, I love,

I love You. Je -

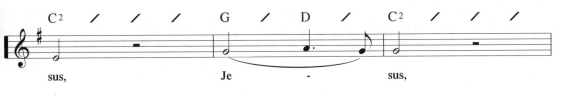

sus, Je - sus,

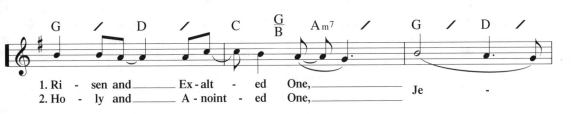

1. Ri - sen and Ex - alt - ed One, Je -
2. Ho - ly and A - noint - ed One,

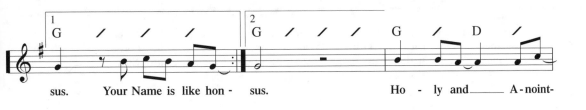

sus. Your Name is like hon - sus. Ho - ly and A - noint-

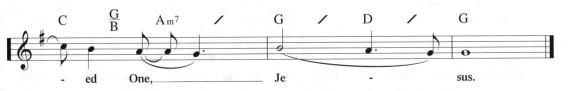

- ed One, Je - sus.

11
The River Is Here

Words and Music by
ANDY PARK

With joy ♩ = ca. 124

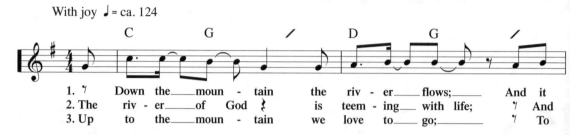

1. Down the moun - tain the riv - er flows; And it
2. The riv - er of God is teem - ing with life; And
3. Up to the moun - tain we love to go; To

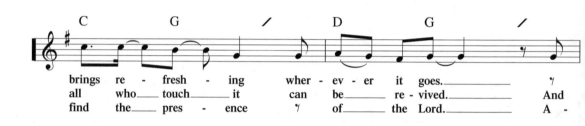

brings re - fresh - ing wher - ev - er it goes.
all who touch it can be re - vived. And
find the pres - ence of the Lord. A -

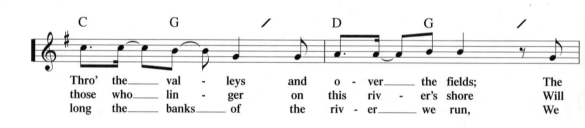

Thro' the val - leys and o - ver the fields; The
those who lin - ger on this riv - er's shore Will
long the banks of the riv - er we run, We

riv - er is rush - ing and the riv - er is here.
come back thirst - ing for more of the Lord. The
dance with laugh - ter giv - ing praise to the Son.

riv - er of God sets our feet a - danc - ing, The

riv - er of God_____ fills our hearts with___ cheer._____ The

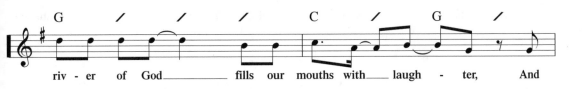

riv - er of God_____ fills our mouths with___ laugh - ter, And

1, 2 (optional)

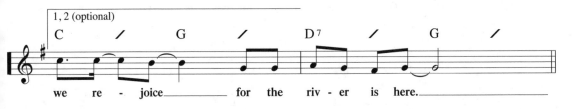

we re - joice_____ for the riv - er is here._____

Instrumental "turn-around"

flute melody

3

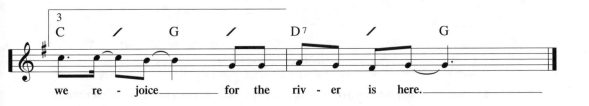

we re - joice_____ for the riv - er is here._____

12   Give Thanks

Words and Music by
HENRY SMITH

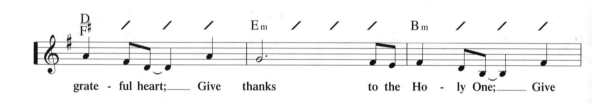

PLEASE NOTE: Copying of this product is NOT covered by CCLI licenses. For CCLI information call 1-800-234-2446.

strong;"   Let the poor say, "I am rich,"   be-cause of

what   the Lord has done   for___ us._____ And

now   let the weak say, "I am strong;"   Let the

poor say, "I am rich,"   be-cause of what   the Lord has

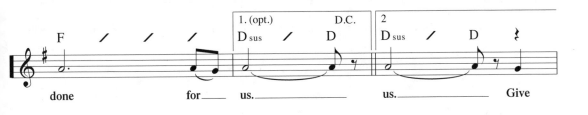

done   for___ us._____ us._____ Give

thanks!_____ Give thanks!_____

13   Step by Step

Words and Music by
DAVID STRASER

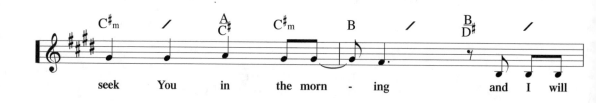

PLEASE NOTE: Copying of this product is NOT covered by CCLI licenses. For CCLI information call 1-800-234-2446.

step by step You'll lead   me and I will

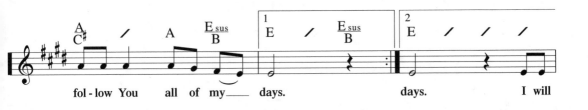

fol - low You all of my   days. days. I will

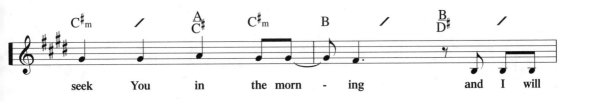

seek You in the morn - ing and I will

learn to walk in Your   way;   And

step by step You'll lead   me and I will

fol - low You all of my   days.

14
All of My Life

Words and Music by
CASSIDY HARRIS

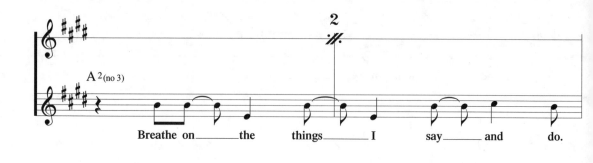

Breathe on_____the things_____I say_____and do.

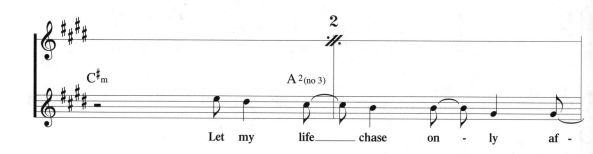

Let my life_____chase on - ly af -

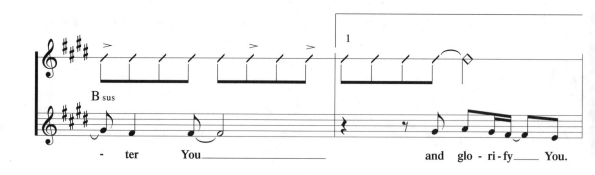

- ter You_____ and glo - ri - fy_____ You.

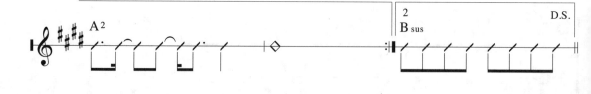

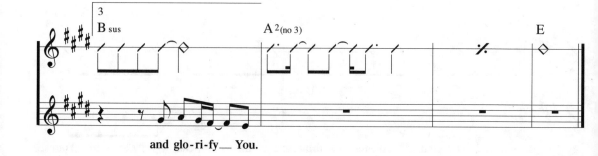

and glo - ri - fy__ You.

Holy, You Are Holy

Words and Music by
BRUCE WICKERSHEIM

16

Be Exalted, O God

Words and Music by
BRENT CHAMBERS

Worshipful ♩ = ca. 90

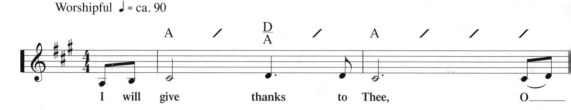

I will give thanks to Thee, O____

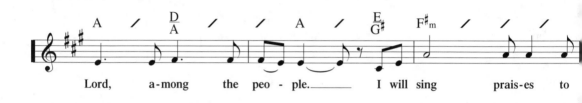

Lord, a-mong the peo-ple.____ I will sing prais-es to

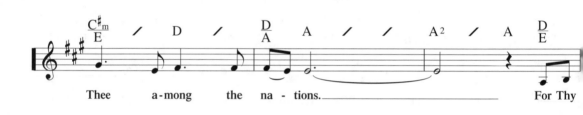

Thee a-mong the na-tions.____ For Thy

stead-fast love is great, is____ great to the

heav-ens,____ And Thy faith-ful-ness, Thy____ faith-ful-ness to____ the

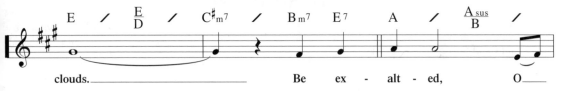

clouds._____ Be ex - alt - ed, O____

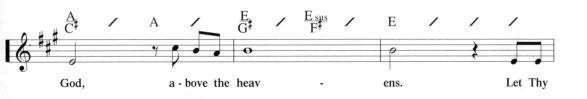

God, a - bove the heav - ens. Let Thy

glo - ry be o - ver all____ the earth._____

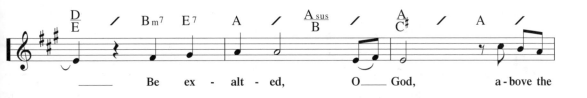

_____ Be ex - alt - ed, O___ God, a - bove the

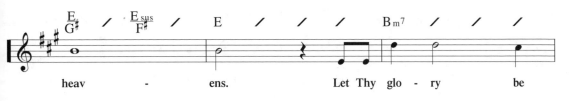

heav - ens. Let Thy glo - ry be

o - ver all____ the earth._____

17

Faithful to Me

Words and Music by
BOB DIEHM

Light and intimate ♩ = ca. 100

I will walk_____ thro' the fire,_____ I will run

_____ and not_____ grow tired._____ For I know_____ You've been faith-

- ful to me._____ Thro' the night.

_____ I have peace,_____ Ev-en tho'_____ I can - not see.

_____ For I know_____ You are faith - ful to me._

18 We Want to See Jesus Lifted High

Words and Music by
DOUG HORLEY

Driving ♩ = ca. 132

We want to see Je - sus lift - ed high,__

A ban - ner that flies__ a - cross__ this land,__

That all men might see__ the truth__ and know__

He is the way__ to heav - en.

We want to see,   we want to see,   We want to see Je -
We're gon-na see,   we're gon-na see,   We're gon-na see Je -

19   In the Secret

Words and Music by
ANDY PARK

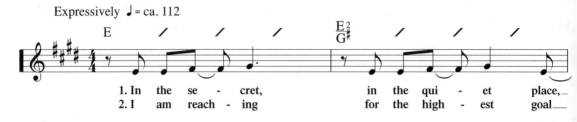

1. In the se - cret, in the qui - et place,
2. I am reach - ing for the high - est goal

In the still - ness
That I might re -

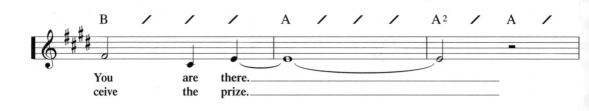

You are there.
ceive the prize.

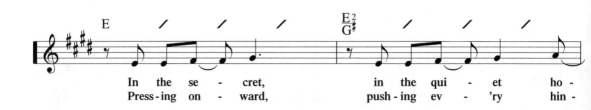

In the se - cret, in the qui - et ho -
Press - ing on - ward, push - ing ev - 'ry hin -

- ur I wait on - ly for You,
- drance a - side, out of my way,

'Cause I want___ to know You more.___

_____ I want to know You,___

I want to hear Your___voice; I want to

know You___ more.___

I want to touch You,___ I want to

see Your___face; I want to know You___ more.___

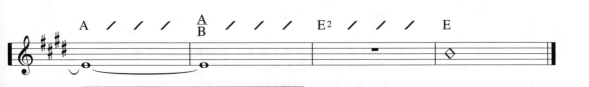

20 There Is Joy in the Lord

Words and Music by
CHERI KEAGGY

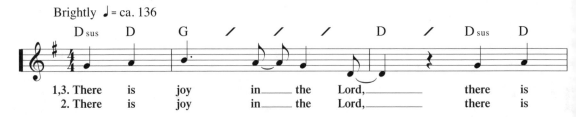

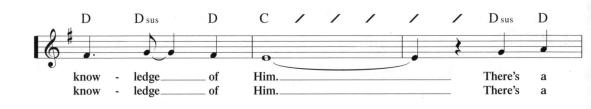

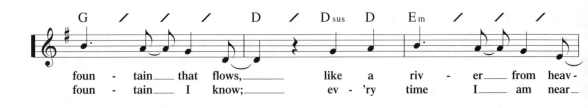

soul._____ All bless - ing____ and hon - or____ are
Lord._____

His,_____ All_____ glo - ry_____ and

pow - er_____ are His._____ Let all

wis - dom_____ and strength be_____ the Lord's in_____ this

place. Let all glo - ry_____ be giv - en_____ to

D.C. al Coda CODA

Him._____ soul.

21 Amazing Love

Words and Music by
GRAHAM KENDRICK

With devotion ♩ = ca. 74

1. My Lord, what love is this
2. And so they watched Him die;
3. And now this love of Christ

that pays
de - spised, so re -
shall flow like

dear - ly; That I,
ject - ed; But O
riv - ers; Come wash

the guilt - y one
the blood He shed
your guilt a - way,

may go free.
flowed for me. A -
live a - gain.

maz - ing love,_____ O what sac - ri - fice,_____

_____ The Son of God,_____ giv'n for

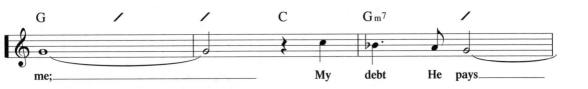

me;_____ My debt He pays_____

_____ and my death He dies,_____ That

I_____ might_____ live,_____ that

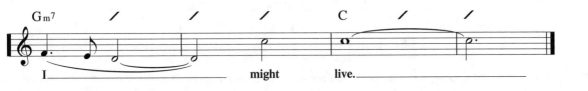

I_____ might live._____

22 Open the Eyes of My Heart

Words and Music by
PAUL BALOCHE

With energy ♩ = ca. 116

O - pen the eyes____ of my heart,____ Lord,_____

o - pen the eyes____ of my heart;_____ I want__ to

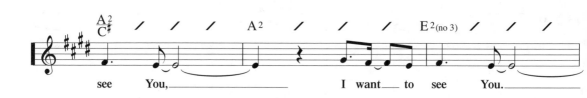

see You,_____ I want__ to see You.

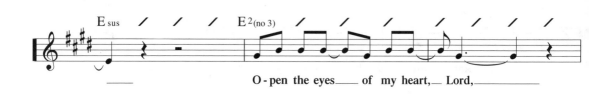

____ O - pen the eyes____ of my heart,__ Lord,_____

o - pen the eyes_____ of my heart;_____ I want____ to

see You,_____ I want_ to see You._____

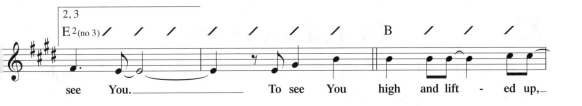

see You._____ To see You high and lift - ed up,__

_____ shin - ing in the light of Your glo - ry.

Pour out__ Your pow'r and love;_____ As we sing ho - ly, ho - ly, ho -

- ly._____ Ho - ly, ho - ly, ho - ly,_____

ho - ly, ho - ly, ho - ly;_____ Ho - ly, ho - ly, ho -

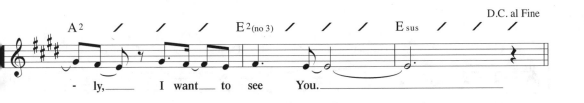

- ly,_____ I want__ to see You._____

23

Every Move I Make

Words and Music by
DAVID RUIS

Ev - 'ry move I make I make in You, You make me— move, Je - sus.

Ev - 'ry breath I take I breath in You.———

Ev - 'ry step I take I take in You, You are my— way, Je - sus.

Ev - 'ry breath I take I breath in You.———

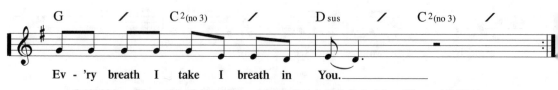

24 The Heart of Worship

Words and Music by
MATT REDMAN

25

Love You So Much

Words and Music by
RUSSELL FRAGAR

Heartfelt ♩ = ca. 80

D DM7

Hear these prais - es from a grate - ful heart;____

GM7

Each time I think of You,____ the prais - es start.____ Love You

Last time to Coda ⊕

**F#m Em F#m Em Em
A A A A D D**

so much,____ Je - sus;____ Love You so much.____

**A Em7 D DM7
A**

Lord I love You, my soul sings;____

GM7

In Your pres - ence,____ car-ried on Your wings.____ Love You

**F#m Em F#m Em Em
A A A A D D**

so much,____ Je - sus;____ Love You so much.____

26 I've Found Jesus

Words and Music by
MARTIN SMITH

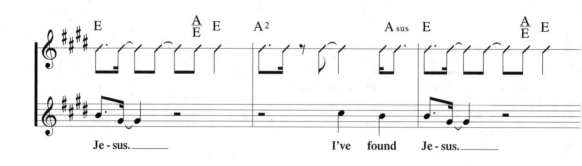

Je - sus.＿＿＿＿＿＿ I've found Je - sus.＿＿＿＿＿＿

I've found Je - sus.＿＿＿＿＿＿ I've found

2nd time to Coda

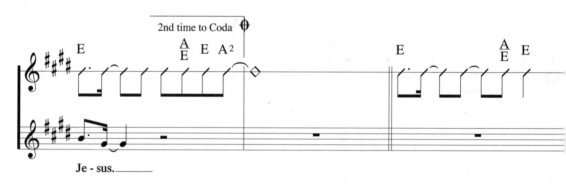

Je - sus.＿＿＿＿＿

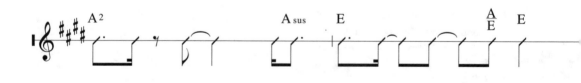

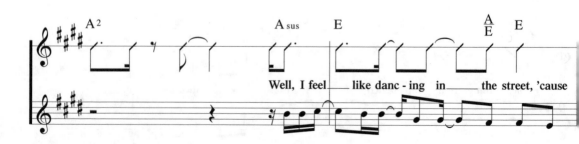

Well, I feel＿＿ like danc - ing in＿＿＿ the street, 'cause

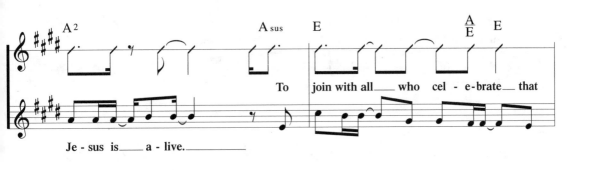

To join with all___ who cel - e-brate___ that

Je - sus is___ a - live.___

Well, the joy of God___ is in___ this town, 'cause

Je - sus is___ a - live.___

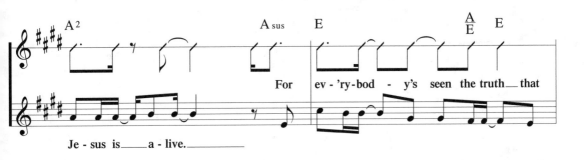

For ev - 'ry-bod - y's seen the truth___ that

Je - sus is___ a - live.___

D.S. al Coda CODA

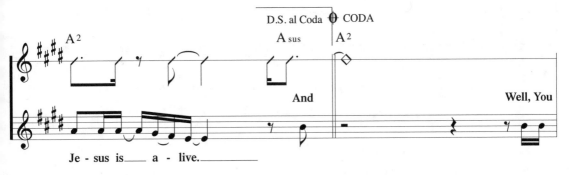

And

Well, You

Je - sus is___ a - live.___

lift - ed me___ from where___ I was,___ set my feet___ up - on a Rock,___

E/F#   A²
Hum-bled that___ You ev-en knew___ a-bout___ me,_____ Now

C#m7   E/A
I have chos-en to___ be-lieve,___ be-liev-ing that You've chos-en me.___

E/G#   A²
I was lost___ but now I'm found.___

I've   found

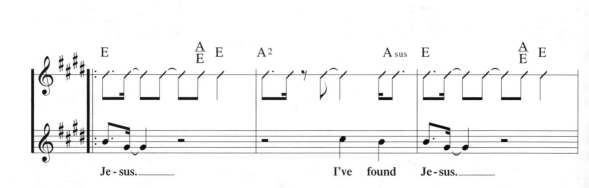

E   A/E E   A²   A sus E   A/E E
Je-sus.___   I've found Je-sus.___

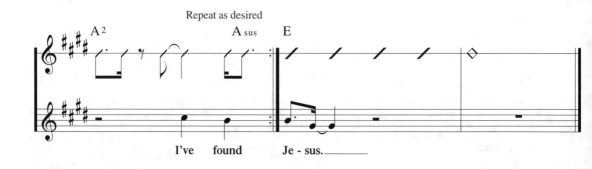

Repeat as desired
A²   A sus   E
I've   found   Je-sus.___

Desire of My Heart

Words and Music by
MARTY PARKS

Fervently ♩ = ca. 88

O De-sire of my heart, O De-light of my

soul; You fill me com-plete - ly,

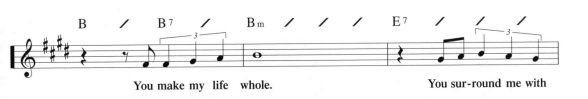

You make my life whole. You sur-round me with

joy by the love on - ly You im -

part: I will praise You for - ev - er

O De - sire of my heart.

28   We Have Come to Worship Him

Words and Music by
CHERI KEAGGY

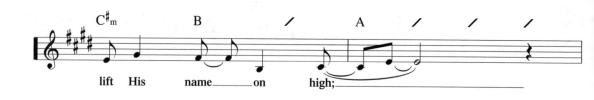

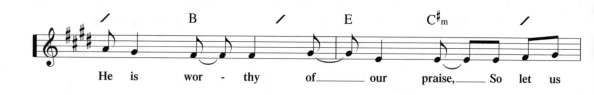

He is___ the King___ of Kings,_____
He is___ the Prince___ of Peace,_____

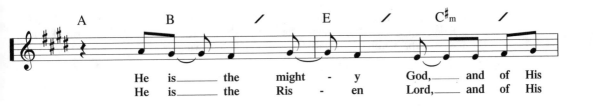

He is___ the might - y God,___ and of His
He is___ the Ris - en Lord,___ and of His

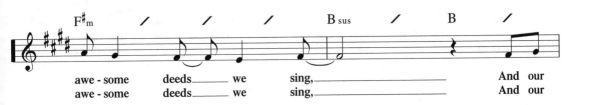

awe - some deeds___ we sing,_____ And our
awe - some deeds___ we sing,_____ And our

high - est praise___ to Him___ we bring._____
high - est praise___ to Him___ we bring._____

_____ We__ have come___ to wor - ship Him._____

We___ have come___ to wor - ship Him._____

29

Shout to the North

Words and Music by
MARTIN SMITH

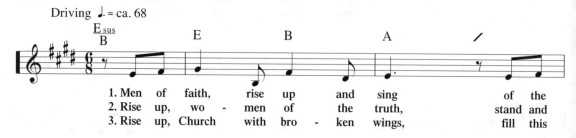

1. Men of faith, rise up and sing of the
2. Rise up, wo-men of the truth, stand and
3. Rise up, Church with bro-ken wings, fill this

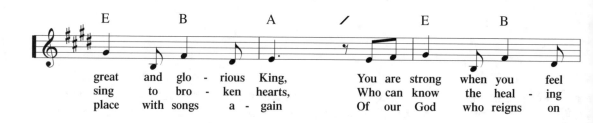

great and glo-rious King, You are strong when you feel
sing to bro-ken hearts, Who can know the heal - ing
place with songs a - gain Of our God who reigns on

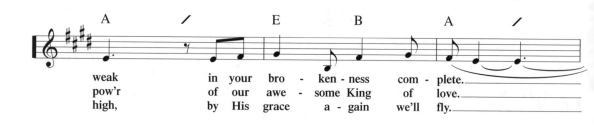

weak in your bro - ken-ness com - plete._____
pow'r of our awe - some King of love._____
high, by His grace a - gain we'll fly._____

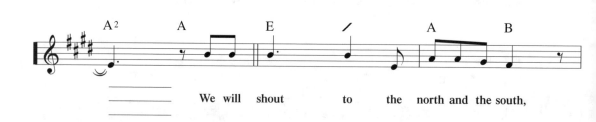

_____ We will shout to the north and the south,

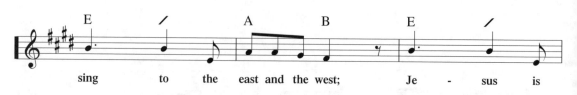

sing to the east and the west; Je - sus is

Sav - ior to all, Lord of Heav-en and earth._____

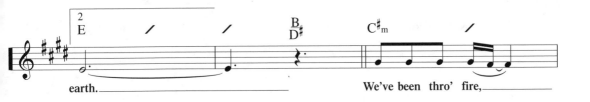

earth._____ We've been thro' fire,_____

we've been thro' rain, We've been re-fined_____ by the

pow'r of His name; We've fal - len deep-er_____

in love with You, You've burned the truth_____ on our

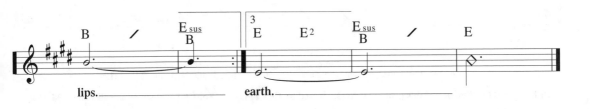

lips._____ earth._____

30

King of Kings

Words and Music by
DAVE MOODY

Sovereign Lord

31

Words and Music by
TOM FETTKE

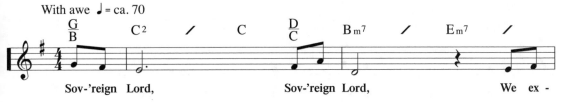

Sov-'reign Lord, Sov-'reign Lord, We ex-

alt Your ho-ly name, Sov-'reign Lord. Cre-

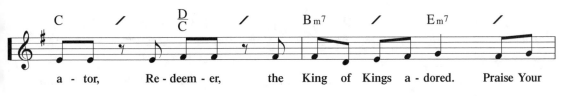

a-tor, Re-deem-er, the King of Kings a-dored. Praise Your

name, praise Your ho-ly name, Sov-'reign

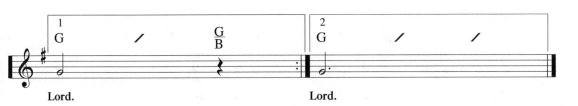

Lord. Lord.

32 I Give You My Heart

Words and Music by
REUBEN MORGAN

With devotion ♩ = ca. 92

This is my_____ de-sire,_____ to hon - or

You: Lord, with all_____ my heart_____ I wor-ship You._

_____ All I have_____ with-in_____

_____ me, I give You praise:

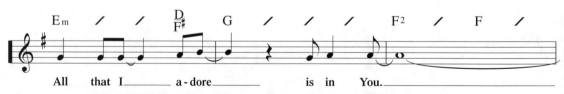

All that I_____ a-dore_____ is in You._____

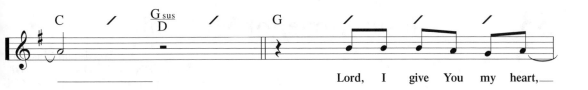

Lord, I give You my heart, ___

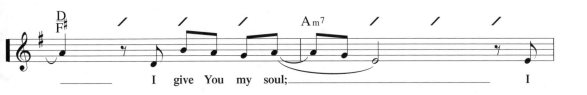

___ I give You my soul; _____ I

live for You a - lone. _____ Ev - 'ry breath that I take, ___

_____ ev - 'ry mo - ment I'm ___ a - wake; _____ Lord,

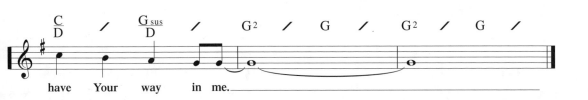

have Your way in me. _____

33 Jesus, Lover of My Soul

Words and Music by
JOHN EZZY, DANIEL GRUL
and STEPHEN MCPHERSON

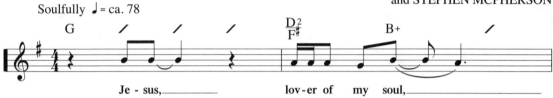

Je - sus,_____ lov-er of my soul,_____

Je - sus,_____ I will nev-er let You go:_____

You've tak-en me_____ from the mir - y clay,_____

You've set my feet up-on_____ the rock_____ and now I know:

I love You, I need You,

tho' my world will fall,____ I'll nev-er let____ You go;_____

My Sav - ior, my clos-est Friend,_____

Repeat ending   D.C. or D.S.

I will wor-ship You____ un - til the ver - y end._____

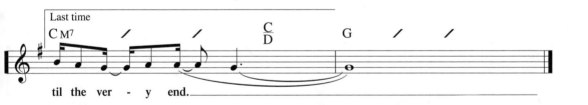

Last time

til the ver - y end._____

34 I Will Exalt Your Name

Words and Music by
JEFFREY B. SCOTT

With energy ♩ = ca. 92

Lyrics:
I will ex-alt Your name,___ I will ex-alt Your name.___ I will ex-alt___ Your name,___ O my God.___ I will ex-alt Nev-er be-fore,___ nev-er a-gain

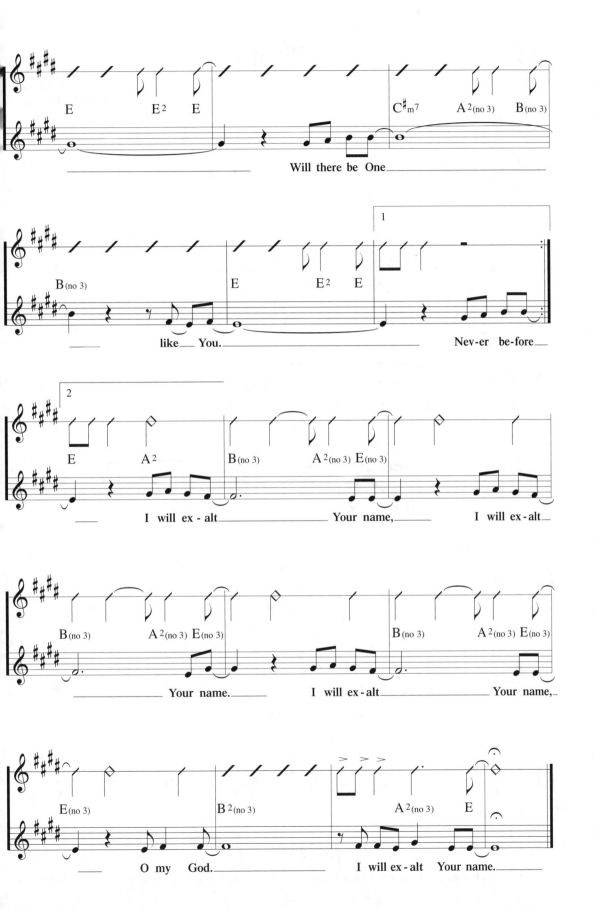

35 Glorify

Words and Music by
LINDA BARNDHILL

36 # Come, Now Is the Time to Worship

Words and Music by
BRIAN DOERKSEN

Come, now is the time____ to wor - ship.__

_____ Come, now is the time____ to give__

_____ your heart. Come,

just as you are____ to wor - ship._____

Come, just as you are____ be - fore_____ your

God.   Come.

One day, ev - 'ry tongue will con - fess_____ You are God._____

One day, ev - 'ry knee_____ will bow._____

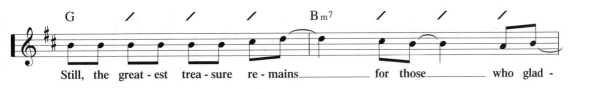

Still, the great - est trea - sure re - mains_____ for those_____ who glad -

- ly choose_____ you now._____

Come.

37 Lamb of God

Words and Music by
TWILA PARIS

With conviction ♩ = ca.64

1. Your on - ly Son no sin to hide, But You have
2. Your gift of love they cru - ci - fied, They laughed and
3. I was so lost I should have died, But You have

sent Him from Your side To walk up - on this guilt - y
scorned Him as He died, The hum - ble King they named a
brought me to Your side To be led by Your staff and

sod And to be - come the Lamb of God.
fraud And sac - ri - ficed the Lamb of God.
rod, And to be called a lamb of God.

O Lamb of God, sweet Lamb of God, I love the

ho - ly Lamb of God. O wash me in His pre - cious

blood, (1,2) My Je - sus Christ, the Lamb of God.
(3) Till I am just a lamb of God.

I Exalt Thee

Words and Music by
PETE SANCHEZ, JR.

39   The Love of Christ

Words and Music by
MARTY PARKS

Peacefully ♩ = ca. 88

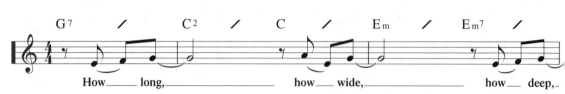

How___ long,_____ how__ wide,_____ how__ deep,__

_____ how__ high_____ Is the love of Christ,_____

_____ the love of Christ._____ How__ long,__

_____ how__ wide,_____ how__ deep,_____ how__ high,__

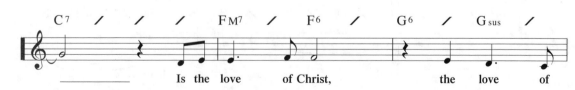

_____ Is the love of Christ, the love of

C / / / Fine C⁷ / / / G/F F / /

Christ. Sur - pass - ing___ all know - ledge,___ Grant - ing

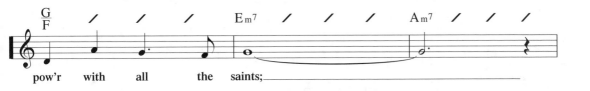

G/F / / / Em⁷ / / / Am⁷ / / /

pow'r with all the saints;_____

Dm⁷ / / / G⁷ / / / C² / C /

Fill - ing us,_____ fill - ing us.

C⁷ / / / G/F F / / G/F / / /

And out of___ His rich - es___ He es - tab - lish - es our

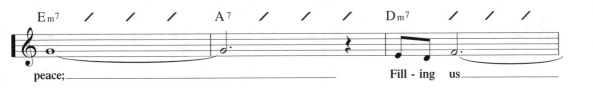

Em⁷ / / / A⁷ / / / Dm⁷ / / /

peace;_____ Fill - ing us___

D.C. al Fine

Dm⁷ / / / C/G / Gsus / Gsus /

___ with the full - ness of God.

40   O the Glory of Your Presence

Words and Music by
STEVE FRY

O the glo - ry_____ of Your pres - ence.____

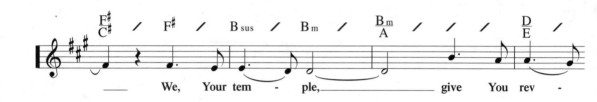

____ We, Your tem - ple,_____ give You rev -

'rence._____ So a - rise to Your rest and be

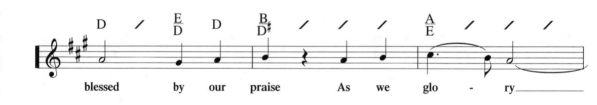

blessed by our praise As we glo - ry____

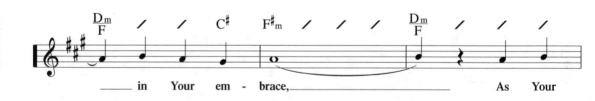

____ in Your em - brace,_____ As Your

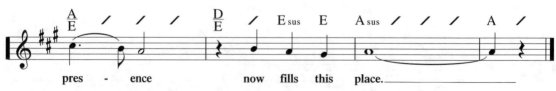

pres - ence now fills this place.____

Lord, Reign in Me

Words and Music by
BRENTON BROWN

Driving ♩ = ca. 96

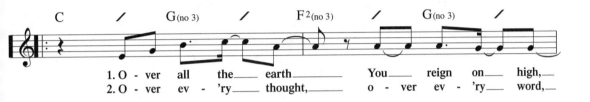

1. O - ver all the earth You reign on high,
2. O - ver ev - 'ry thought, o - ver ev - 'ry word,

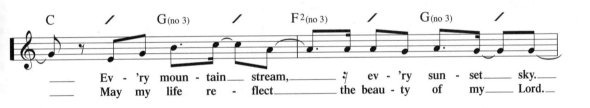

Ev - 'ry moun - tain stream, ev - 'ry sun - set sky.
May my life re - flect the beau - ty of my Lord.

But my one re - quest, Lord, my on - ly aim
'Cause You mean more to me than an - y earth - ly thing,

is that You'd reign in me a - gain.
So won't You reign in me a - gain.
Lord, reign in me,

reign in Your pow'r. O-ver all my dreams in my dark - est hour.

You are the Lord of all I am, So won't You

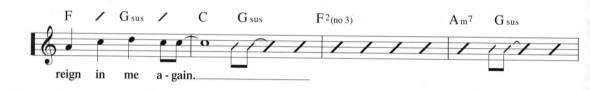

reign in me a - gain.

O - ver all the earth You reign on high,

Ev - 'ry moun - tain stream, ev - 'ry sun - set sky.

But my one re - quest, Lord, my on - ly aim

_____ is that You'd reign in me a-gain. Lord, reign in___ me,___

___ reign in Your___pow'r.___ O-ver all my___dreams___ in my dark-est hour.

You are the Lord___ of all I am,_____ So won't You

reign in me a-gain. Won't You reign in me a-gain.___

42   Lord, You Have My Heart

Words and Music by
MARTIN SMITH

43 Refiner's Fire

Words and Music by
BRIAN DOERKSEN

With conviction ♩ = ca. 76

1. Pu - ri - fy_____ my heart,_____ let me be as
2. Pu - ri - fy_____ my heart,_____ cleanse me from with -

gold and pre - cious sil - ver.
in and make me ho - ly.

Pu - ri - fy_____ my heart,_____ let me be as
Pu - ri - fy_____ my heart,_____ cleanse me from my

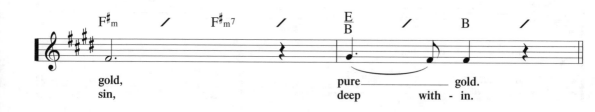

gold, pure_____ gold.
sin, deep with - in.

Re - fin - er's fire,_____

My heart's___ one de - sire_____ is to

be ho - ly, set___ a - part___ for You__

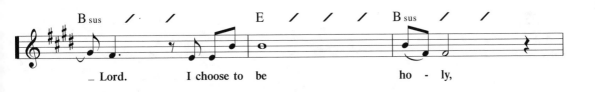

___ Lord. I choose to be ho - ly,

set___ a - part___ for___ You_____ my mas - ter,

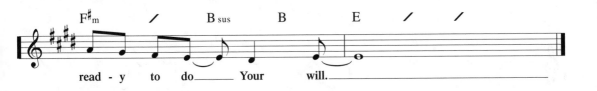

read - y to do___ Your will._____

44 Message of the Cross

Words and Music by
MARTIN SMITH

With zeal ♩ = ca. 102

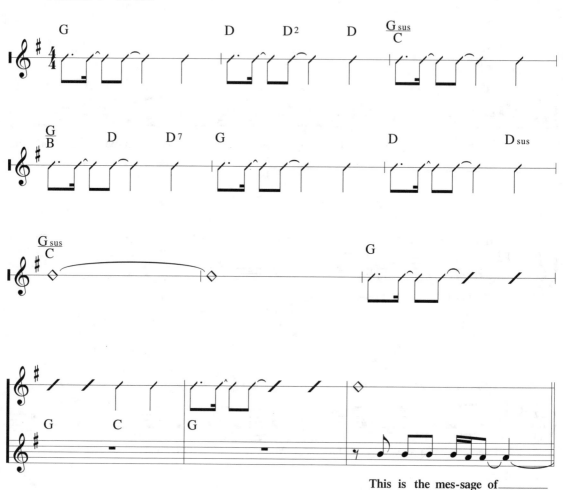

_the cross,_____ That we can__ be free,

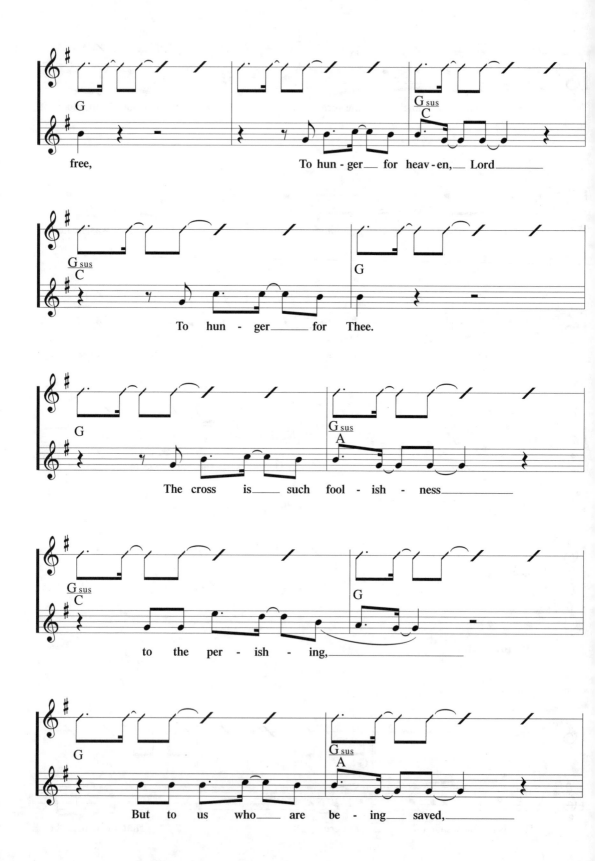

45 Great Is the Lord

Words and Music by
MICHAEL W. SMITH
and DEBORAH SMITH

Vibrantly ♩. = ca. 60

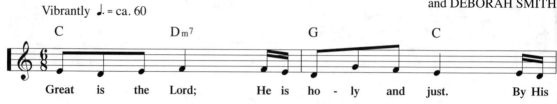

Great is the Lord; He is ho - ly and just. By His

pow - er we trust in His love.

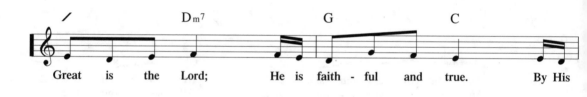

Great is the Lord; He is faith - ful and true. By His

mer - cy He proves He is love.

Great is the Lord and wor - thy of glo - ry!
(D.S.) Great are You, Lord, and wor - thy of glo - ry!

PLEASE NOTE: Copying of this product is NOT covered by CCLI licenses. For CCLI information call 1-800-234-2446.

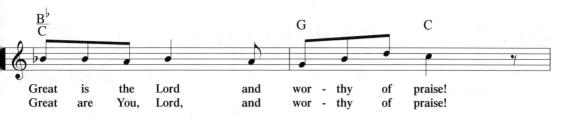

Great is the Lord and wor - thy of praise!
Great are You, Lord, and wor - thy of praise!

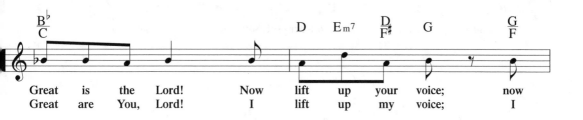

Great is the Lord! Now lift up your voice; now
Great are You, Lord! I lift up my voice; I

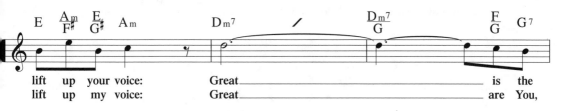

lift up your voice: Great_____ is the
lift up my voice: Great_____ are You,

Lord!_____ Great_____
Lord!_____ Great_____

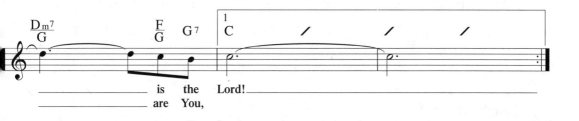

_____ is the Lord!_____
_____ are You,

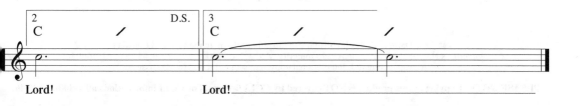

Lord! Lord!_____

46

The Potter's Hand

Words and Music by
DARLENE ZSCHECH

With devotion ♩ = ca. 104

Beau-ti-ful Lord,_____ won-der-ful Sav-ior, I know for sure_____

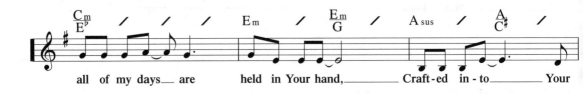

all of my days__ are held in Your hand,_____ Craft-ed in-to_____ Your

per - fect plan. I'm cap-tured by_____ Your

ho - ly call - ing, Set me a-part_____ I know You're draw - ing

me to Your - self;_____ Lead me, Lord,___ I pray._____

Take me, _____ mold me, _____

use me, _____ fill me; _____ I give my life_____

to the Pot - ter's hand._____

Call me, _____ guide me, _____ lead me,_____ walk be -

side me;_____ I give my life_____ to the Pot - ter's hand.__

Repeat verse   D.C. | Repeat chorus   D.S. | Ending

47 Hungry (Falling on My Knees)

Words and Music by
KATHRYN SCOTT

With energy ♩ = ca. 88

1. Hun - gry I__ come to__ You for__ I know__ You sat - is - fy.
2. Bro - ken I__ run to__ You for__ Your arms__ are o - pen wide.

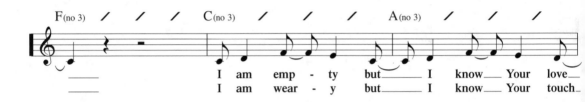

I am emp - ty but__ I know__ Your love__
I am wear - y but__ I know__ Your touch__

does not__ run dry.__ And so I wait for You,__
re - stores__ my life.__

So I wait for You.__ I'm fall -

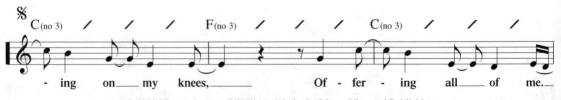

- ing on__ my knees,__ Of - fer - ing all__ of me.

Je - sus,___ You're all___ this heart___ is liv-ing for.___

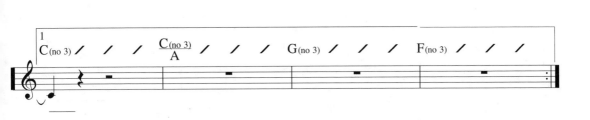

I'm fall -___

And so I wait for You.___ So I

wait   for   You.___   So I   wait   for   You.__

___   So I   wait   for   You._____

___   I'm   fall__ ___ Yes, You are,___ yes, You are.____   I'm   fall-

- ing   on__ my   knees,____   Of - fer - ing   all__ of   me.__

___   Je - sus,__ You're   all__ this   heart____ is liv-ing   for.__

Hun - gry I___ come to___ You for___ I know___

___ You sat - is - fy._____ I am emp - ty but___

___ I know___ Your love_____ does not___ run dry._____

48

You Are the King

Words and Music by
BRUCE GREER

Majestically ♩ = ca. 92

We lift up the gates;___ we o - pen the doors___ That

You may come in,___ that You may come in.___ We

o - pen our hearts___ to You Might - y Lord___ That

You may come in,___ that You may come in.___

You are the King of Glo - ry, Ho - san - na,___

ho - san - na! You are the King of Glo - ry,

Ho - san - na,___ ho - san - na!

More than Worthy

49

Words and Music by
CHRISTINE HAYS

50

We Fall Down

Words and Music by
CHRIS TOMLIN

To Worship You

51

KEN BIBLE

TOM FETTKE and
RICHARD KINGSMORE

52 Be Magnified

Words and Music by
LYNN DESHAZO

With awe ♩ = ca. 84

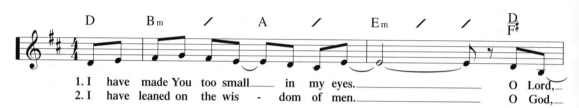

1. I have made You too small in my eyes. O Lord,
2. I have leaned on the wis - dom of men. O God,

for - give me. And I have be - lieved in a lie
for - give me. And I have re - spond - ed to them

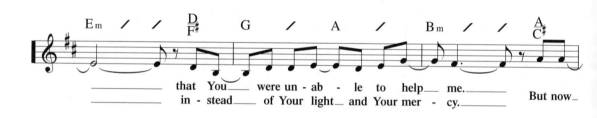

that You were un - ab - le to help me.
in - stead of Your light and Your mer - cy. But now

O Lord, I see my wrong. Heal my heart and show

Your - self strong. And in my eyes and with my song, O

Lord, be mag - ni - fied,_____ O___ Lord, be mag - ni -

fied._____ Be mag - ni - fied,_____ O Lord,_____

You are high - ly___ ex - alt - ed.   And there is noth-ing You___

___ can't do,_____ O Lord,___ my eyes___ are on You,_____ Be mag - ni -

fied,_____ O___ Lord, be mag - ni - fied._____

53 Knowing You

Words and Music by
GRAHAM KENDRICK

With devotion ♩ = ca. 66

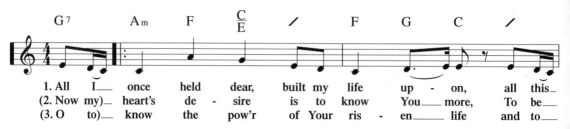

1. All I___ once held dear, built my life up - on, all this___
(2. Now my)___ heart's de - sire is to know You___ more, To be___
(3. O to)___ know the pow'r of Your ris - en___ life and to

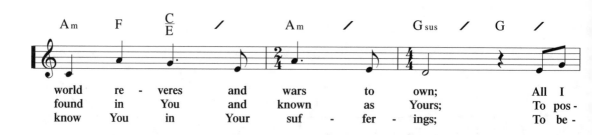

world re - veres and wars to own; All I
found in You and known as Yours; To pos-
know You in Your suf - fer - ings; To be-

once thought gain I have count - ed___ loss; spent and___
sess by faith what I could not___ earn, All sur -
come like You in Your death, my___ Lord, So with

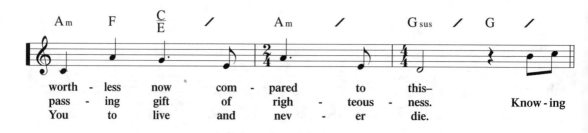

worth - less now com - pared to this— Know - ing
pass - ing gift of righ - teous - ness.
You to live and nev - er die.

You, Je-sus, know-ing You, there is no great-er___

thing. You're my all, You're the best,___ You're my

joy, my righ-teous-ness, and I love You, Lord.___ 2. Now my___
3. O to___

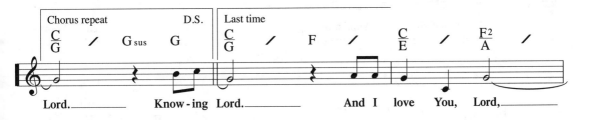

Lord.___ Know-ing Lord.___ And I love You, Lord,___

___ and I love You, Lord,___ and I

love You, Lord.___

54 Thank You for Saving Me

Words and Music by
MARTIN SMITH

1. Thank You for sav - ing me; ′ what__ can I
2. Mer - cy and grace are mine, for-giv-en is my

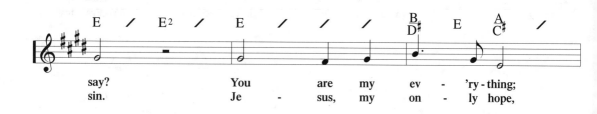

say? You are my ev - 'ry - thing;
sin. Je - sus, my on - ly hope,

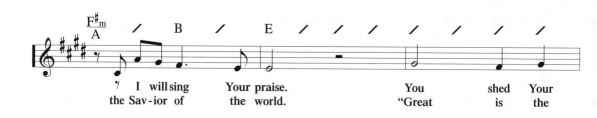

′ I will sing Your praise. You shed Your
the Sav-ior of the world. "Great is the

blood for me; ′ what__ can I say?
Lord," we cry, God, let Your king - dom come.

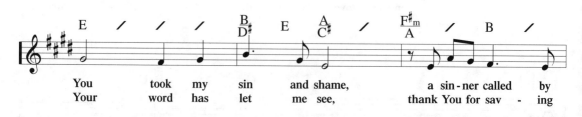

You took my sin and shame, a sin - ner called by
Your word has let me see, thank You for sav - ing

There Is a Redeemer

55

Words and Music by
MELODY GREEN

Like a hymn ♩ = ca. 80

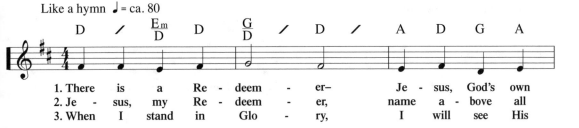

1. There is a Re - deem - er— Je - sus, God's own
2. Je - sus, my Re - deem - er, name a - bove all
3. When I stand in Glo - ry, I will see His

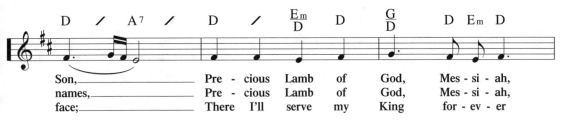

Son,____ Pre - cious Lamb of God, Mes - si - ah,
names,____ Pre - cious Lamb of God, Mes - si - ah,
face;____ There I'll serve my King for - ev - er

Ho - ly One.
O____ for sin - ners slain.
in____ that ho - ly place. Thank You, O my

Fa - ther, for giv - ing us Your Son,____ And

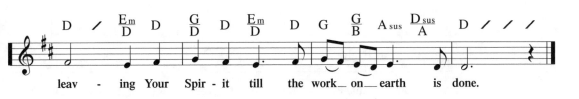

leav - ing Your Spir - it till the work__on__earth is done.

56 We Thank You for Your Presence

Words and Music by
MARTY NYSTROM

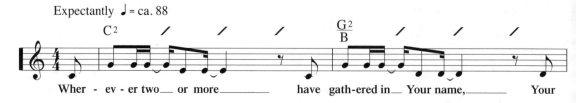

Wher - ev - er two__ or more_____ have gath-ered in__ Your name,_____ Your

pres - ence__ O Lord,_____ will be there in that place._____ So we

have-n't an - y doubt_____ You're here a-mong__ us now,_____

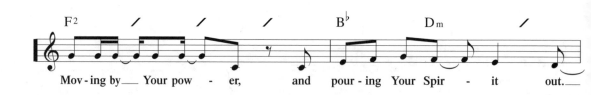

Mov-ing by__ Your pow - er, and pour-ing Your Spir - it out.___

_____ Lord, we thank You_____ for Your pres - ence,_____ For Your

Spir - it in___ this place; We will bold - ly___ come be-

fore You,___ Draw-ing near to Your throne__ of grace._____ Lord, we

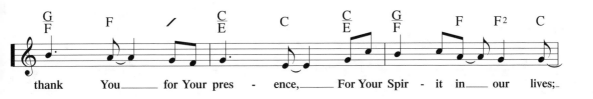

thank You_____ for Your pres - ence,_____ For Your Spir - it in___ our lives;_

_____ We en-throne You on___ our prais - es,_____ And we

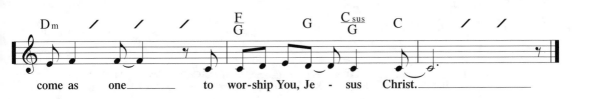

come as one_____ to wor-ship You, Je - sus Christ._____

57   Above All

Words and Music by
LENNY LEBLANC
and PAUL BALOCHE

With feeling ♩ = ca. 64

A-bove all pow - ers,   a-bove all kings,   A-bove all

na - ture and all cre - at - ed things;   A-bove all

wis - dom and all the ways of man,

You were here be-fore the world be - gan.   A-bove all

king - doms,   a-bove all thrones,   A-bove all

58   Better Is One Day

Words and Music by
MATT REDMAN

Brightly ♩ = ca. 92

1. How love-ly is Your dwell-ing place,   O Lord Al-might-
(2. One) thing I ask and I would seek: to see Your beau-

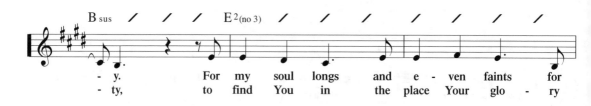

-y.   For my soul longs and e - ven faints for
-ty,   to find You in the place Your glo - ry

You._____   For here my heart is sat - is - fied
dwells._____   One thing I ask and I would seek;

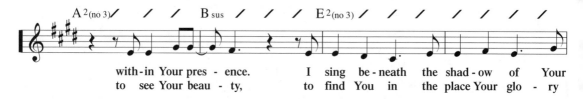

with-in Your pres - ence.   I sing be - neath the shad - ow of Your
to see Your beau - ty,   to find You in the place Your glo - ry

wings._____   Bet-ter is one day in Your courts, bet-ter is
dwells._____

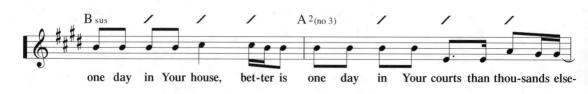

one day in Your house, bet-ter is one day in Your courts than thou-sands else-

59 Ancient of Days

Words and Music by
JAMIE HARVILL
and GARY SADLER

Spirited ♩ = ca. 102

Bless - ing____ and hon - or,   glo - ry____ and pow - er

Be un - to____ the An - cient of Days.____

From ev - 'ry na - tion,   all of____ cre - a - tion,

Bow be - fore____ the An - cient of Days.____

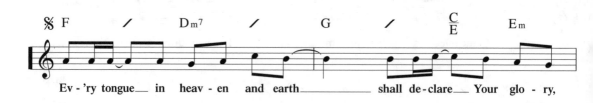

Ev - 'ry tongue__ in heav - en and earth____ shall de - clare__ Your glo - ry,

Ev - 'ry knee____ shall bow at Your throne____ in wor - ship;

60

Ever Faithful

Words and Music by
BRUCE WICKERSHEIM

With devotion ♩ = ca. 64

Yes - ter - day_____ and to-day_____ and for-ev-

- er You're the same,_____ Ev - er con - stant, nev - er chang-

- ing is Your grace._____ Yes - ter-day__

_____ and to - day_____ ev - er faith - ful is Your name,__

_____ I'll lay down_____ my life, O Lord,_____ as a gift of

praise.　　　　Ev - er　faith -

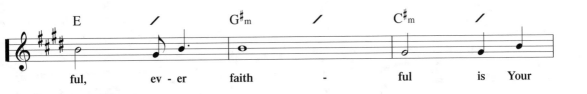

ful,　　ev - er　faith　-　　ful　is　Your

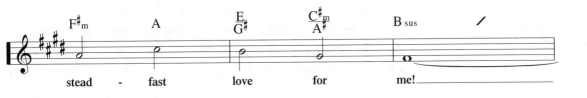

stead - fast　love　for　me!＿＿＿＿＿

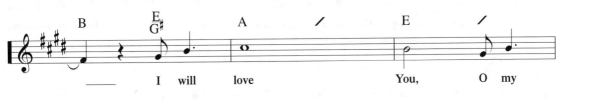

＿＿＿＿　I　will　love　　　You,　　O　my

Je　-　　sus,　　For - ev - er

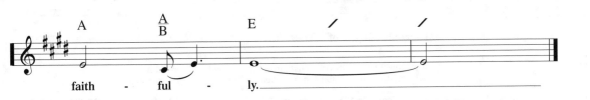

faith - ful - ly.＿＿＿＿＿＿＿＿＿

61

I Could Sing of
Your Love Forever

Words and Music by
MARTIN SMITH

With passion ♩ = ca. 86

O - ver the moun-tains and the sea   Your riv - er runs with love for me,

and I will o - pen up my heart,___ and let the Heal - er set me free.

I'm hap - py to be in the truth, and I will dai - ly lift my hands

for I will al - ways sing of when Your love come down.___

___ I could sing of Your love___ for - ev - er,

I could sing of Your love___ for - ev - er,___

62 We Have Come to Worship You

Words and Music by
MARTY PARKS

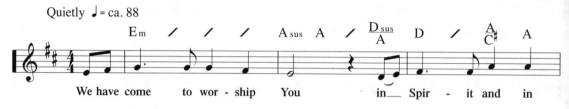

We have come to wor-ship You in Spir-it and in

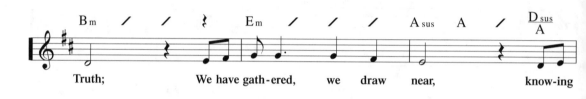

Truth; We have gath-ered, we draw near, know-ing

You will meet us here. We have come to wor-ship

You in Spir-it and in Truth; Ho-ly

Lord, meet us here.

You Are Holy; I Come in Silence 63

Words and Music by
KEN BIBLE

Quietly ♩ = ca. 90

You are ho - ly; I come in si - lence.

You are wise, Lord; I come to hear.

You are God; I come to o - bey

You. You are love; I come to draw near.

You are love; I come to draw near.

64 He Is Exalted

Words and Music by
TWILA PARIS

With praise ♩. = ca. 60

He is ex - alt - ed, the King is ex - alt - ed on high._____ I will

praise_____ Him. He is ex - alt - ed, for - ev - er ex - alt - ed and

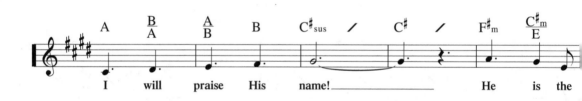

I will praise His name!_____ He is the

Lord._____ For - ev - er His truth shall reign._____

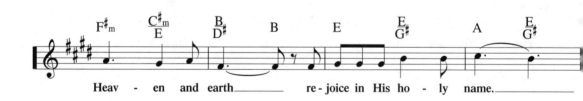

Heav - en and earth_____ re - joice in His ho - ly name._____

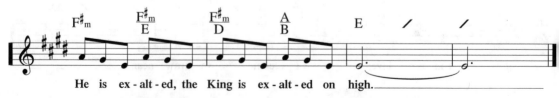

He is ex - alt - ed, the King is ex - alt - ed on high._____

More Love, More Power

Words and Music by
JUDE DEL HIERRO

Passionately ♩ = ca. 72

66 You Are My King

Words and Music by
BILLY JAMES FOOTE

With feeling ♩ = ca. 66

I'm for-giv - en_____ be-cause You were_ for-sak - en._____

I'm ac-cept - ed,_____ You were_ con-demned._____

I'm a-live_ and well,_ Your spir - it is_ with-in_ me Be -

cause You died_ and rose_ a-gain._____

A - maz-ing love,_____ how_ can it be_____

That You,_ my King_ would die_ for me?_____

67 Breathe

Words and Music by
MARIE BARNETT

Worshipfully ♩ = ca. 68

1. This is the air I breathe,
2. This is my dai - ly bread,

this is the air I breath;
this is my dai - ly bread;

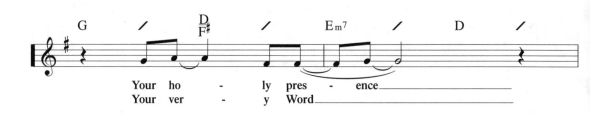

Your ho - ly pres - ence
Your ver - y Word

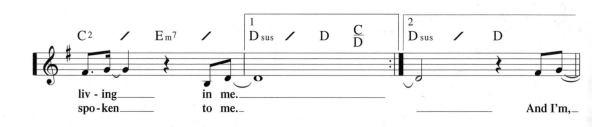

liv - ing in me.
spo - ken to me. And I'm,

I'm des-p'rate for

PLEASE NOTE: Copying of this product is NOT covered by CCLI licenses. For CCLI information call 1-800-234-2446.

C / Em / Dsus / D / G² / D/F♯ /

_ You._____ And I'm,_____

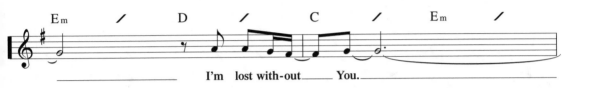

Em / D / C / Em /

_____ I'm lost with-out_____ You._____

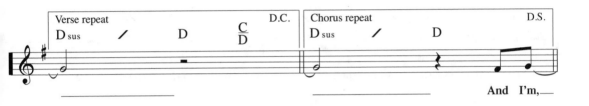

Verse repeat   D.C. | Chorus repeat   D.S.
Dsus / D / C/D | Dsus / D

_____ | _____ And I'm,__

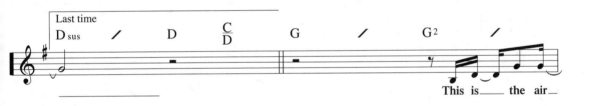

Last time
Dsus / D / C/D / G / G² /

_____ This is___ the air_

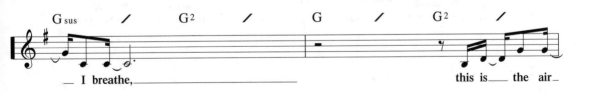

Gsus / G² / G / G² /

_ I breathe,_____ this is___ the air_

Gsus / G² / G / G² / G / /

_____ I_____ breathe._____

68 The Happy Song

Words and Music by
MARTIN SMITH

Deliriously ♩ = ca. 116

O I could sing un - end - ing songs Of how you saved my soul,_____ Well, I could dance a thou - sand miles Be - cause of Your great love._____

My heart is burst - ing, Lord,_____ to tell of all__ You've done,_____ Of how You've changed my life_____ and wiped a-way__ the past;_____

See How Mercy

69

Words and Music by
GARY SCHMIDT

Expressively ♩ = ca. 64

70 Forever

Words and Music by
CHRIS TOMLIN

With life ♩ = ca. 120

Give thanks to the Lord,_____ our

God and_____ King;_____ His love en - dures_____ for - ev -

G 2(no 3)

car - ry___ on,_____ His love en - dures__ for - ev - er, Sing

CODA

G 2(no 3)

- er. For - ev - er God___ is___ faith - ful, For - ev -

$\frac{G\,2(no\,3)}{E}$ ・ ・ ・ $\frac{G\,2(no\,3)}{D}$

- er God___ is strong._____ For - ev - er God___ is with__

C 2(no 3)

__ us, For - ev - er, and ev - er, for - ev -

G 2(no 3) $\frac{G\,2}{E}$

- er.___

$\frac{G\,2}{D}$ C 2(no 3)

71

You Alone

Words and Music by
DAVID CROWDER
and JACK PARKER

With devotion ♩ = ca. 134

You are the on - ly One I

need, I bow all of me at Your

feet, I wor - ship You a -

lone.

You have giv - en me more than

I could ev - er have want - ed, And I

_____ want to give You my _____ heart and my _____

_____ soul. _____

You _____ a-lone _____ are _____ Fa - ther _____ and You _____

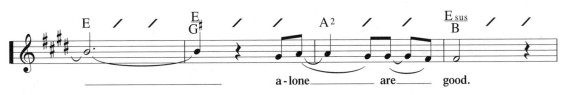

_____ a - lone _____ are _____ good.

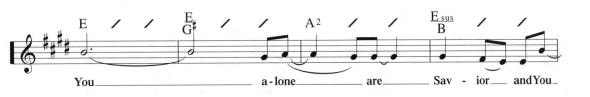

You _____ a - lone _____ are _____ Sav - ior _____ and You _____

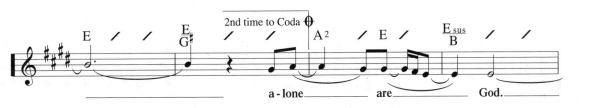

2nd time to Coda

_____ a - lone _____ are _____ God.

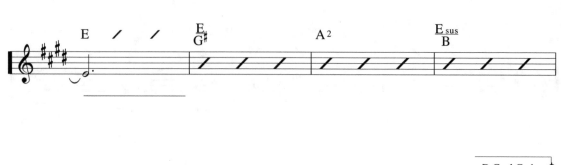

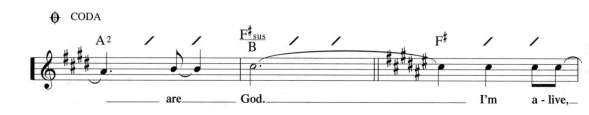

_____ are_____ God._____ I'm   a - live,_

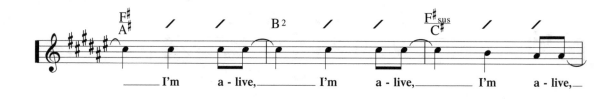

_____ I'm   a - live,_____ I'm   a - live,_____ I'm   a - live,_

_____ I'm   a-live,_____ I'm   a-live,_____ I'm   a-live,_____ I'm   a-live,_

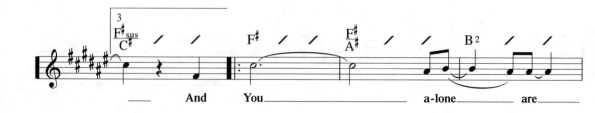

_____   And   You_____ a-lone_____ are_

Fa - ther and You _____ a-lone _____ are _____

good. You _____ a-lone _____ are _____

Sav - ior and You _____ a-lone _____ are _____

God. God. _____

72   Trading My Sorrows

Words and Music by
DARRELL EVANS

Brightly ♩ = ca. 120

I'm trad - ing___ my sor - rows,___
I'm trad - ing___ my sick - ness,___

I'm trad - ing___ my shame,___
I'm trad - ing___ my pain,___

I'm lay - ing___ them down for the joy of___ the
I'm lay - ing___ them down for the joy of___ the

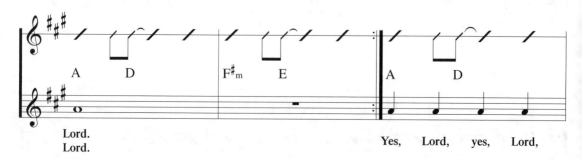

Lord.
Lord.   Yes, Lord, yes, Lord,

yes,   yes,   Lord;————   Yes,   Lord,   yes,   Lord,

yes,   yes,   Lord;——   Yes,   Lord,   yes,   Lord,   yes,   yes,   Lord,   A-men.

I am pressed— but not— crushed,   per - se -

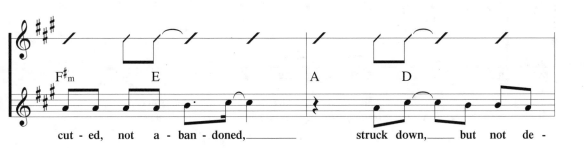

cut - ed,   not   a - ban - doned,————   struck down,——   but   not   de -

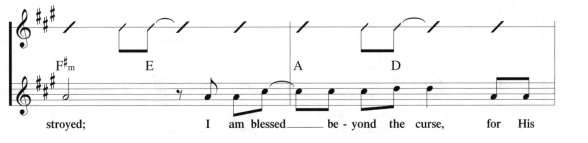

stroyed;   I   am   blessed————   be - yond   the   curse,   for   His

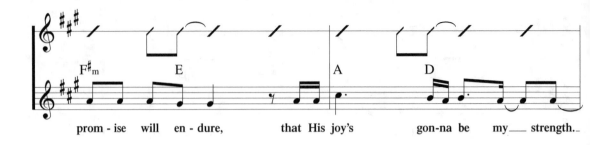

prom - ise will en - dure, that His joy's gon-na be my____ strength.__

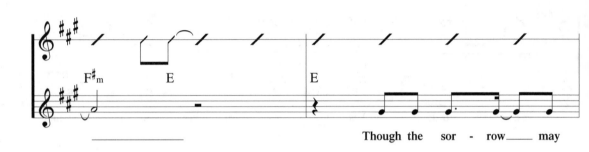

_____ Though the sor - row____ may

last for__ the night, His joy comes with the morn - ing._____

I'm trad - ing____ my sor - rows,____
I'm trad - ing____ my sick - ness,____

I'm trad - ing____ my shame,____
I'm trad - ing____ my pain,____

I'm lay - ing____ them down for the joy of____ the
I'm lay - ing____ them down for the joy of____ the

Lord.
Lord.   Lai,

lai, lai,____ lai, lai, lai,____ lai, lai, lai,____ lai, lai;   Lai,

lai, lai,____ lai, lai, lai,____ lai, lai, lai,____ lai, lai;_____   Lai,

lai, lai,____ lai, lai, lai,____ lai, lai, lai,____ lai, lai, lai, lai.____

73 Firm Foundation

Words and Music by
NANCY GORDON
and JAMIE HARVILL

With joy ♩ = ca. 112

Je - sus, You're my firm foun - da - tion,_____

I know I can stand_____ se - cure;_____

Je - sus, You're my firm foun - da - tion,_____

I put my hope in Your ho - ly Word,_____

Fine last time

I put my hope in Your ho - ly Word._____

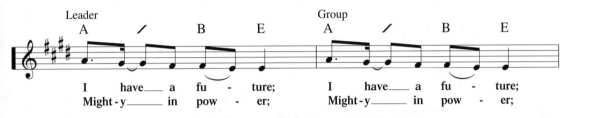

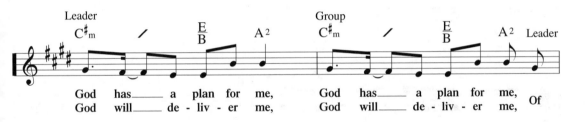

74 We Proclaim Your Righteousness

Words and Music by
ED HOGAN

Who can count the won - ders from Your____ hand?_____

Won - der - ful and match - less is Your____ plan._____

You have made the sac - ri - fi - cial of - fer - ing,

We will raise our voice____ to You and____ sing. We pro -

claim Your righ - teous - ness,____ O Lord, We will

speak of Your faith - ful - ness___ and sav - ing___ grace;

O - pen up___ our hearts to sing Your love___ and truth, We pro -

claim Your righ - teous - ness___ in the ho - ly

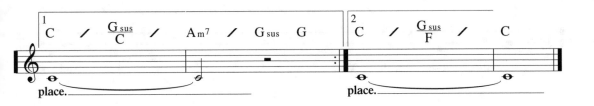

place.___ place.___

75

Let My Words Be Few

Words and Music by
BETH and MATT REDMAN

With emotion ♩ = ca. 84

You are God in heav-en and here am I on earth.

So I'll let my words be few.

Je - sus, I am so

in love with You. And I'll

stand in awe of You,

Yes, I'll stand   in awe_____ of You,

_____   And I'll let_____ my words_____ be few.___

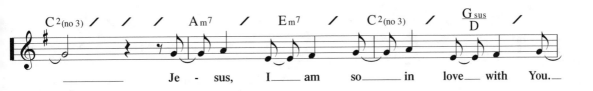

_____   Je - sus,   I____ am   so_____ in   love___ with   You.___

_____   The sim-plest of__ all   love_

_ songs   I want_____ to bring_____ to You._____

So I'll   let_____ my words_____be few_____

Je - sus, I__ am so__ in love__ with You.

And I'll / And I'll

stand in awe_____ of You._____

1. Yes I'll
2. So I'll
3. Yes I'll

And I'll let_____ my words_____ be few._____ Je -

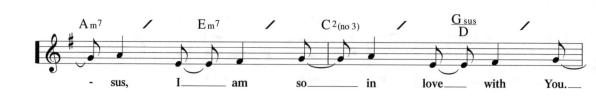

- sus, I__ am so_____ in love__ with You.__

Index of Keys and Meter Signatures

This index is provided for the use of worship leaders who want to plan their own worship sequences, or medleys. By referring to the keys and meter signatures, such medleys can be planned with the proper balance of continuity and variety.

Topical Index
with Keys

Alphabetical Index

(with Keys)